How Do Trees Grow?

Sharon McConnell

Rosen
REAL
READERS

The Rosen Publishing Group, Inc.
New York

Published in 2001 by The Rosen Publishing Group, Inc.
29 East 21st Street, New York, NY 10010

Book Design: Haley Wilson

Photo Credits: Cover, title page, pp. 2–3, 7, 14–16 © SuperStock; pp. 4, 14 © Tony Stone Images; p. 8 © T. Zuidema/ The Image Works; pp. 11–12 © International Stock.

ISBN: 0-8239-8136-3
6-pack ISBN: 0-8239-8538-5

Manufactured in the United States of America

Contents

4

Old and Tall

Trees are the oldest living things on Earth. Some trees are 4,000 years old! Some trees are as tall as buildings. Even the oldest and tallest trees were once tiny seeds that dropped from another tree.

Trees are the biggest plants on Earth.

The Parts of Trees We Can See

All trees have a main body or **trunk**. Many branches grow from the trunk, and leaves grow from the branches. Leaves come in many different sizes and shapes. The leaves that grow on pine trees are called **needles**.

Trees keep growing for as long as they live.

Where Are the Roots?

Roots take in water and **minerals** that the tree needs to live and grow. Roots also help hold the soil together and keep the tree from falling over. Roots start at the bottom of the tree and then grow underground.

Roots can be three times as long as a tree's branches.

Tree Sap

Trees make a **sugary** water called **sap**. Sap carries food and water to the different parts of a tree. Some people collect the sap from maple trees in the spring. The sap is then turned into maple **syrup**.

Metal cans are used to catch sap from maple trees in the spring.

How Do Leaves Help Trees?

As leaves grow, they take **carbon dioxide** from the air. Leaves use sunlight to change water and carbon dioxide into sugar. Sugar is food for the trunk, branches, and roots of the tree. Leaves also make **oxygen** and let it out into the air. We need oxygen to breathe.

In the fall, leaves cannot get enough sunlight to live. They change color and fall off the trees.

Planting New Trees

Many trees are cut down every year so we can build things, like houses, from their wood. We do not want to run out of trees. It is important for us to plant new trees to take the place of the trees we cut down.

Glossary

carbon dioxide A gas that trees take in from the air and use to make food for themselves.

mineral A natural thing that comes from Earth's soil and helps trees grow.

needle The leaf of a pine tree.

oxygen A gas that trees let out into the air. People and animals cannot live without it.

root The part of a tree that grows mostly underground.

sap The sugary water that carries food and water to the different parts of a tree.

sugary Sweet and sticky.

syrup A thick, sweet liquid. We put maple syrup on pancakes.

trunk The main body of a tree.

Index